FAITH THROUGH OUR EYES

30-Day Devotional Written By Kids

Dominick Winston Kule-Thomas
and
Diana Isabelle Kule-Thomas

Edited by
Diana Iyamide Kule-Thomas

COPYRIGHT PAGE

Faith Through Our Eyes: 30-Day Devotional Written by Kids
© 2025 by Dominick Winston Kule-Thomas and Diana Isabelle Kule-Thomas
All rights reserved. No part of this publication may be reproduced, distributed, or transmitted in any form or by any means, including photocopying, recording, or other electronic or mechanical methods, without the prior written permission of the publisher, except in the case of brief quotations embodied in critical reviews and certain other noncommercial uses permitted by copyright law.

ISBN: 978-1-7352299-1-1
eBook ISBN: 978-1-7352299-2-8

Library of Congress Control Number: 2025923635
Published by Diana Iyamide Kule-Thomas Publishing
Printed in the United States of America

This devotional is authored by Dominick Winston Kule-Thomas and Diana Isabelle Kule-Thomas. This registration covers the complete text, prayers, and original artwork contained in this book.

Cover design and interior layout © 2025 Diana Iyamide Kule-Thomas Publishing
First Edition – 2025

TABLES OF CONTENTS

Part 1 — Growing With God: Faith In Everyday Life
1. The Helpful Stranger
2. Kindness In The Grocery Aisle
3. Over The Fence, Into Kindness
4. Giving Money To A Beggar
5. Is It "Bad" To Water My Neighbor's Plants?
6. The Tic Tac Thief: A Lesson In Honesty
7. I Traded My Reputation For A Piece Of Chewing Gum
8. When Life Feels Unfair
9. Conviction By The Holy Spirit: What Are The Traits Of Lord Jesus' Disciples?
10. The Israelites' Epic Timeout

Part 2 — Serving With Joy: Living Out Love
11. Our Mission To Help The Homeless
12. Wrapping Christmas Presents For Toy Donations
13. Beach Cleanup Adventure: Our Rainy Day Mission!
14. My Teammates Won, And I'm Cheering Her On!
15. Jumping For A Healthy Heart
16. Roasting S'mores And Scripture
17. Winning The Spelling Bee: What I Learned
18. A Glimpse Of God's Creation, Planet Neptune

TABLES OF CONTENTS

19. Seeing The World Like Lord Jesus, Through My Eyeglasses
20. A Girl's Search For Light While Praising God

Part 3 — Faith & Courage: Trusting God's Plan
21. Moses Stuttered Too
22. True Friendship Or Give-Me Friendship
23. Destiny Challenge Game
24. Taking Care Of My Eyes With God's Help
25. God Healed My Eyes!
26. Hail In Florida?! God Can Do Anything!
27. My First Snow: A Prayer Answered
28. Lost In The Snow: My Phone Gone Forever
29. Rule-Breakers On The Plane
30. We Were Stuck On The Plane: Trusting God's Perfect Timing

WELCOME FROM DOMINICK AND DIANA ISABELLE

We're Dominick and Diana Isabelle, and we're so excited to share our very first devotional with you! We wrote this book from our own experiences—things we've learned at home, at school, and while helping others.

We hope you enjoy reading about the adventures, challenges, and fun moments we've had. Most importantly, we want you to see how God is part of every little thing we do—whether it's helping someone in need, learning from a mistake, or celebrating something exciting.

This devotional is special because it's written by kids, for kids! We want you to know that we're right there with you, sharing stories, asking questions, and learning how to follow God in your everyday life.

We're so happy you're reading our book, and we can't wait for you to explore God's love with us.

— *Dominick & Diana Isabelle*

HOW TO USE THIS DEVOTIONAL

This devotional book is designed to help you think about God's Word and how it applies to your life. Each section has four parts:
1. Memory Verse – Each devotional has a special verse from the Bible to remember and carry with you.
2. Experience – We share a story from our life that teaches a lesson about faith, kindness, or courage.
3. Reflection Questions – These are questions to help you think about what the story means for you and how you can apply it.
4. Prayer – A short prayer to help you talk to God about what you learned and how you can grow closer to Him.

You can read one story each day or pick the ones that catch your eye. You can also write your thoughts, prayers, or experiences in the space below — it's your time to talk with God. Remember, this is your devotion book, so make it personal, fun, and meaningful!

The Helpful Stranger

> HE ANSWERED, "LOVE THE LORD YOUR GOD WITH ALL YOUR HEART AND WITH ALL YOUR SOUL AND WITH ALL YOUR STRENGTH AND WITH ALL YOUR MIND"; AND, LOVE YOUR NEIGHBOR AS YOURSELF.
> LUKE 10:27

Our car broke down in the middle of a busy Costco gas station while my mom was pumping gas!

On November 12, 2023, we stopped at the Costco Station to fill our red car with gas; something unexpected happened. After my mom filled up the tank, the car decided it didn't want to start! So, she went looking for someone to help push the car out of the busy Costco gas station to be towed.

Despite so many cars around that Sunday, no one offered to help. My mom then went to get a Costco employee, but even the employee couldn't push the car alone. That's when the magic happened! Out of the 50 cars lined up, a kind stranger, a real-life good Samaritan, offered to help push the vehicle while Isabelle and I watched the miracle happen.

The good Samaritan asked my mom if she needed help and joined her in pushing the car to the corner parking lot. Luckily, as the car was being moved, it started, and we made it home safely.

Now, Let's Reflect

1. What do you think Dominick and Diana should do?

_____

_____

_____

2. Have you ever found yourself in a situation where you needed help, and it seemed like no one was around?

_____

_____

_____

3. What do you think you would say to the person who stepped up to help and to those who stayed in their cars?

_____

_____

_____

Prayer

Dear God,
Thank you for sending helpful people into our lives when we need them. Help us to be kind and ready to lend a hand to others. Amen.

Kindness In The Grocery Aisle

> JESUS REPLIED, "I AM THE BREAD OF LIFE. WHOEVER COMES TO ME WILL NEVER BE HUNGRY AGAIN. WHOEVER BELIEVES IN ME WILL NEVER BE THIRSTY."
> JOHN 6:35

While waiting in line at the Publix grocery store, a man approached me with a bag of Pasta, asking,

"Do you mind if I go ahead and pay for my one item?" I replied, "Sure." He thanked me, proceeded to pay for his groceries, and walked ahead. My mom, standing behind me, clapped and said, "I am so proud of you for showing him grace and kindness."

Now, Let's Reflect

1. What do you think of the experience of Dominick letting the man go ahead of him?

_____

_____

_____

2. Have you ever been in a situation where someone showed you unexpected kindness?

_____

_____

_____

3. In what ways can you incorporate more grace and kindness into our daily lives?

_____

_____

_____

Prayer
Dear God,
Thank you for the opportunities to show grace and kindness to others. Help me to be mindful of these moments and to approach them with a loving heart. Amen.

Over The Fence, Into Kindness

DO TO OTHERS AS YOU WOULD LIKE THEM TO DO TO YOU.
LUKE 6:31

Have you ever seen someone crying and wanted to make them smile again? That's exactly what I did.

I helped a five-year-old girl at school by getting her ball back when it went over the fence. She was crying because she lost it. A boy next to her had thrown the ball away on purpose and made her sad. Their teacher saw what happened and told him to stop.

Even though it was a small act, it made the little girl so happy. I learned that when we choose kindness, we can turn someone's tears into a smile.

Now, Let's Reflect

1. Have you ever seen someone being unkind to another person? What did you do, or what could you do next time?

_____

_____

_____

2. How do you think the girl felt when she got her ball back?

_____

_____

_____

3. What are some ways we can show kindness and make others feel included and happy at school or when we play?

_____

_____

_____

Prayer

Dear God,
Thank you for helping me do something kind. Please help me to always care for others and stand up for what is right, even when it's hard. Teach me to have a heart like yours—one that loves, helps, and forgives. Amen.

Giving Money To A Beggar

GIVE YOUR GIFTS IN PRIVATE, AND YOUR FATHER, WHO SEES EVERYTHING, WILL REWARD YOU.
MATTHEW 6:4

One day after our yearly doctor's appointment, we saw a man standing by the road asking for help.

He was walking from car to car, hoping someone would give him some loose change. When he came near our car, Mommy asked me, "Diana Isabelle, would you like to give him some of your change?"

I was so happy to help! I gave the man some money, and it made me feel really good inside. I told Mommy that I would love to do it again next time.

Then Mommy explained that when we give to someone in need, we should do it from the heart — not to show off or tell everyone, but to please God.

Now, Let's Reflect
1. How do you feel when you help someone in need?

___

___

___

2. Why does God want us to give quietly and not boast about it?

___

___

___

3. Can you think of one way you can help someone this week?

___

___

___

Prayer
Dear God,
Thank you for blessing me with what I have. Please help me to share with others who need help. Teach me to give with a kind and humble heart, just like Lord Jesus did. Amen.

Is It "Bad" To Water My Neighbor's Plants?

> LET EACH OF YOU LOOK NOT ONLY TO HIS OWN INTERESTS, BUT ALSO TO THE INTERESTS OF OTHERS.
> PHILIPPIANS 2:4

Have you ever done something kind for someone and then wondered if it was the right thing to do?

It was one of the hottest weeks in Florida. There was no rain for the entire week, and the plants in our community garden were dying. So, I decided to water my neighbor's garden because all the plants looked dead. As I was doing it, I looked up to the heavens and said, **"Am I wrong for watering my neighbor's plants?"**

What if God is blessing you not because of what you are doing, but because of what others are secretly doing for you? Just like me watering other people's plants so they blossom.

Now, Let's Reflect

1. Why is it important to help others, even if they don't know you're helping them?

_____

_____

_____

2. Can small acts of kindness, like watering plants, create a big impact?

_____

_____

_____

3. What are some other ways you can help your neighbors or community?

_____

_____

_____

Prayer

Dear God,
Thank you for the opportunity to help others. Please guide me to be kind and generous, even when no one is watching. Help me to understand that small acts of kindness can make a big difference. Amen.

The Tic Tac Thief: A Lesson In Honesty

WHOEVER WALKS IN INTEGRITY WALKS SECURELY, BUT WHOEVER TAKES CROOKED PATHS WILL BE FOUND OUT.
PROVERBS 10:9

Here's the problem: When my mom is unloading groceries from the shopping cart into the car trunk, my sister Diana Isabelle always reaches for my mom's Tic Tac mints and takes them. She'll share four pieces with me and keep four for herself—the same amount Mom gives us when we ask.

Every time she takes them, she gets caught, and Mom says I'm an **accomplice** in the crime of stealing. That's because Mom always catches Diana Isabelle and me red-handed, sucking on the mints and laughing.
Do you think I'm an **accomplice**, or is my mom right?

Now, Let's Reflect

1. What does it mean to be an accomplice? Think about what it means to be involved in something, even if you didn't start it.

___

___

___

2. Is it still wrong to take something without permission, even if you share it?

___

___

___

3. How can you make better choices next time?
   Think about what you can do differently next time to avoid being part of the problem.

___

___

___

Prayer

Dear God,
Thank you for teaching me about making good choices and being honest. Help me to understand the difference between right and wrong, and guide me to make decisions that please You. Help us to always ask for permission and to respect what belongs to others. Amen.

I Traded My Reputation For A Piece Of Chewing Gum

WHOEVER WALKS IN INTEGRITY WALKS SECURELY, BUT WHOEVER TAKES CROOKED PATHS WILL BE FOUND OUT.
PROVERBS 10:9

Have you ever done something just to impress a friend, and it didn't go as planned?

One day, my friend Diego dared me to walk up to a girl and use a cool pickup line to talk to her. He promised me a piece of chewing gum if it worked. Instead of playing along, I decided to be honest and told the girl about Diego's plan. She didn't want to talk to me and hid behind her friends.
Talk about embarrassing! When I told my mom what happened, she surprised me by buying a whole case of gum to share with Diego and my other friends the next day. She reminded me that being honest was more important than trying to impress people.

Now, Let's Reflect

1. Have you ever felt embarrassed when something didn't go as planned? How did you handle it?

_____

_____

_____

2. How can honesty change the way others feel about us and the way we feel about ourselves?

_____

_____

_____

3. What does it mean to be a good friend? How do our choices affect our friendships?

_____

_____

_____

Prayer

Dear God,
Help me to be honest in everything I do, even when it's hard or embarrassing. Teach me to be a good friend who lifts others up and makes the right choices. Thank you for loving me just as I am. Amen.

When Life Feels Unfair

> IN EVERYTHING I DID, I SHOWED YOU THAT BY THIS KIND OF HARD WORK WE MUST HELP THE WEAK, REMEMBERING THE WORDS THE LORD JESUS HIMSELF SAID: IT IS MORE BLESSED TO GIVE THAN TO RECEIVE.
> ACTS 20:35

Have you ever felt like life just was not fair?

One Sunday, that's exactly how I felt when I didn't win the gift being raffled at church. I was so upset that I cried and threw a fit right there on the ground, causing such a scene that my mom was called to pick me up from Sunday School.

Mommy took me aside, walked with me, and sat down to explain the difference between exchanging gifts and the act of giving from the heart. What my Sunday School teacher didn't know is that just the day before, I had given two birthday gifts to a friend, and on Sunday, I had donated toys to the church for Toy Express at Christmas. I was hoping to be rewarded, but when that didn't happen, I felt very sad.

After my anger faded, my mom walked me back to Sunday School to apologize to the teachers for disrupting the service.

Now, Let's Reflect

1. Have you ever expected something in return for doing something good?
How did you feel when it didn't happen?

_____

_____

_____

2. Why is it important to give without expecting anything in return?

_____

_____

_____

3. How can you handle your feelings when things don't go your way?

_____

_____

_____

Prayer

Dear God,
Thank you for teaching me the importance of giving from my heart without expecting anything in return. Help me to be patient and understanding when things don't go the way I want. Please guide me to always choose kindness and to remember that true blessings come from loving and helping others. Amen.

Conviction By The Holy Spirit: What Are The Traits Of Lord Jesus' Disciples?

> GREATER LOVE HAS NO ONE THAN THIS: TO LAY DOWN ONE'S LIFE FOR ONE'S FRIENDS.
> JOHN 15:13

One day, as I sat down to read, the Holy Spirit asked me a question:
"What do you think about Lord Jesus' disciples?"

I paused for a moment and thought, "Hmm... I think Lord Jesus' disciples represent different character traits that we all possess."

We all have friends who betray us, friends who lie, and friends who deny that they hang out with us. Some friends unfriend us, while others stay by our side. There are friends we pray with, friends we eat and laugh with, and friends who are there when we cry.

Some friends listen to our advice, while others don't. From my perspective, all of Lord Jesus' disciples symbolize behaviors and traits that we all carry. Whichever of these traits you identify with, I pray that the Lord is with you.

Now, Let's Reflect

1. Which of the disciples' traits do you see in yourself or your friends?

_____

_____

_____

2. How do these traits affect your relationship with others and with God?

_____

_____

_____

3. How can you ask God to help you strengthen the positive traits and overcome the negative ones?

_____

_____

_____

Prayer

Dear God,
Thank you for showing me the traits of Your disciples and how they reflect the qualities we see in ourselves and others. Help me to recognize the good traits and strengthen them, while also guiding me to overcome the negative ones. May I always strive to be a better friend and follower of you. Amen.

The Israelites' Epic Timeout

AND YOUR CHILDREN WILL BE LIKE SHEPHERDS, WANDERING IN THE WILDERNESS FOR FORTY YEARS. IN THIS WAY, THEY WILL PAY FOR YOUR FAITHLESSNESS, UNTIL THE LAST OF YOU LIES DEAD IN THE WILDERNESS. "BECAUSE YOUR MEN EXPLORED THE LAND FOR FORTY DAYS, YOU MUST WANDER IN THE WILDERNESS FOR FORTY YEARS-A YEAR FOR EACH DAY, SUFFERING THE CONSEQUENCES OF YOUR SINS. THEN YOU WILL DISCOVER WHAT IT IS LIKE TO HAVE ME FOR AN ENEMY."
NUMBERS 14:33-34

Late one night, just before diving into my dreams, I turned to my mom after our usual Bible study and prayers. Why did the Israelites have to wander in the wilderness for 40 years?"

My Mom hit me with a scenario: "Imagine, kiddo, you're in a time-out at school, and the moment you are free, you throw a punch in the hallway and make another kid's nose bleed. What do you think your teacher would do?"

I answer. "They will give me an even longer time-out, maybe till night or until I promise to behave."

"Absolutely right," Mom nodded. " Picture me as your parent, picking you up, and your teacher spills the beans. I would let the punishment roll, even if it takes till nighttime or, in the Israelites' case, 40 years later."

So, Diana, the Israelites took a detour in the desert because they didn't follow the rules after leaving Egypt. **God gave them an EPIC TIMEOUT- 40 years of learning in the wilderness.**

Now, Let's Reflect

1. What lessons can we learn from the Israelites' **"TIMEOUT"** in the wilderness about the consequences of our actions and the importance of obedience?

_____

_____

_____

2. How does the idea of a **"TIMEOUT"** connect with God's discipline, and what role does patience play in understanding and accepting the consequences of our behavior?

_____

_____

_____

3. In our own lives, when faced with challenges or difficult situations, how can we apply the concept of learning from mistakes and allowing time for growth and change, just as the Israelites did during their 40-year journey?

_____

_____

_____

Prayer
Dear God,
Thank you for guiding us through the stories of the Israelites and teaching us valuable lessons. Help us to learn from our mistakes, understand the consequences, and grow stronger through your love and guidance. Amen.

Our Mission To Help The Homeless

> THE KING WILL REPLY, "TRULY I TELL YOU, WHATEVER YOU DID FOR ONE OF THE LEAST OF THESE BROTHERS AND SISTERS OF MINE, YOU DID FOR ME."
> MATTHEW 25:40

Have you ever wondered how a small act of kindness can make a big difference?

One Saturday, we had the chance to volunteer at our church and help deliver care packages to the homeless in Fort Lauderdale. We woke up early and arrived at the church by 8:00 am, ready to get to work. We packed up carts with toothpaste, toothbrushes, deodorant, washcloths, socks, and shaving essentials for those in need. After packing 100 bags, I lost count!

In Fort Lauderdale, we handed out cold water and care packages to everyone, from little children as young as three to entire families and individuals in need. We even got to talk with the people we were helping, and they shared their wisdom and stories with us. When we finished, we returned to the church to put away the water cooler and cart we used to deliver the care packages.

Now, Let's Reflect

1. How do you think the care packages we made helped the people who received them?

_____
_____
_____

2. Why is it important to listen to the stories and wisdom of those we help?

_____
_____
_____

3. What small acts of kindness can you do in your community to make a big difference?

_____
_____
_____

Prayer

Dear God,
Thank you for giving us the chance to help others. Please bless those who received the care packages and guide us to continue spreading kindness and love wherever we go. Amen.

Wrapping Christmas Presents
For Toy Donations

> EACH OF YOU SHOULD GIVE WHAT YOU HAVE DECIDED IN YOUR HEART TO GIVE, NOT RELUCTANTLY OR UNDER COMPULSION, FOR GOD LOVES A CHEERFUL GIVER.
> 2 CORINTHIANS 9:7

Have you ever tried to wrap a gift and found it trickier than you thought?

Last Christmas, I volunteered at our church to help wrap gifts for the Toy Express donation. There were lots of children who came with their parents to help out. My job was to wrap Christmas presents, but it was not as easy as I thought! The tape kept getting stuck on my hands and the wrapping paper, and my mom had to help me a few times to get it right. Meanwhile, Dominick was in charge of decorating the Christmas trees and hanging red and gold ornaments on the branches.

Even though wrapping the gifts was challenging, I had so much fun knowing that these presents would bring joy to other children. It was a special way to spread Christmas cheer and show God's love.

Now, Let's Reflect

1. Why do you think giving gifts to others, especially those in need, is important?

_____

_____

_____

2. How did it feel to work with others, even when things didn't go perfectly?

_____

_____

_____

3. What's one way you can help someone this Christmas, even if it's something small?

_____

_____

_____

Prayer

Dear God,
Thank you for the chance to bring joy to others during Christmas. Help us to remember that even small acts of kindness, like wrapping a gift, can show your love. Give us patience and a joyful heart as we serve others. Amen.

Beach Cleanup Adventure: Our Rainy Day Mission!

THE EARTH IS THE LORD'S, AND EVERYTHING IN IT, THE WORLD, AND ALL WHO LIVE IN IT.
PSALMS 24:1

Have you ever turned an ordinary day into something extraordinary?

That's what Diana and I did when we joined our church's Beach Cleanup mission!

We picked up 92 lbs of trash from Hollywood Beach! It was so much fun! I love cleaning. We started cleaning at 8:00 am and kept going until 10:00 am, even when it started raining so hard that we had to leave. We were soaked, but it was all for the glory of God and to show others that serving God can be done in many different ways. We look forward to our monthly volunteer activities! I'm so excited to see what we will do next month!

We hope our dedication inspires you to get involved in charitable projects and shows how important it is to protect our oceans and marine life.

Now, Let's Reflect
1. How do you think picking up trash at the beach helps God's creation?

_____

_____

_____

2. Can you think of other ways to serve God in your everyday life?

_____

_____

_____

3. How did it feel to work together with others for a good cause, even when it started to rain?

_____

_____

_____

Prayer
Dear God,
Thank you for the beautiful world you created. Help us to take care of it and serve you in everything we do. Give us the courage to step out and make a difference, even when it is tough. Amen.

My Teammates Won, And I'm Cheering Her On!

> LET EACH OF YOU LOOK NOT ONLY TO HIS OWN INTERESTS, BUT ALSO TO THE INTERESTS OF OTHERS.
> PHILIPPIANS 2:4

Have you ever worked on a project where everyone's ideas came together differently?

In my Aerospace (flight) class, we were given the challenge to build a moon landing project. The first step was to sketch the design and then present the model we planned to build. But before we could move on to construction, our sketches had to be evaluated to decide which one was the best.

I was really proud of my sketch. It was detailed and included a lot of explanations for people to read and understand. My partner's sketch, on the other hand, looked amazing with bright colors and a polished presentation, but it lacked some key details. She wasn't very confident about winning, even though she had put in a lot of effort.

When the results were announced, I was surprised—but happy—to hear her name called as the winner!

I turned to her and said, "Congratulations!" She looked completely shocked, but I could tell she was proud of her work.

This experience taught me that success isn't always about perfection; it's about doing your best and having others recognize the hard work you've put in. It's also about celebrating others, even when you don't come out on top.

Now, Let's Reflect

1. How do you feel when someone else wins, even if you worked hard too?

_____

_____

_____

2. Why is it important to encourage and support others, even in competition?

_____

_____

_____

3. What's one way you can show kindness and celebrate someone's success this week?

___

___

___

Prayer
Dear God,
Thank you for teaching me to celebrate the successes of others. Help me to work hard in all I do and to encourage my friends, even when things don't go my way. Let me always put kindness and teamwork first. Amen.

Jumping For A Healthy Heart

> DO YOU NOT KNOW THAT YOUR BODIES ARE TEMPLES OF THE HOLY SPIRIT, WHO IS IN YOU, WHOM YOU HAVE RECEIVED FROM GOD? YOU ARE NOT YOUR OWN; YOU WERE BOUGHT AT A PRICE. THEREFORE HONOR GOD WITH YOUR BODIES.
> 1 CORINTHIANS 6:19-20

Have you ever jumped rope with your friends? Did you know it can help keep your heart healthy?

February is Heart Healthy Month, and my school organizes an event called **Jump Rope for Heart**. On this special day, we wear pink or red heart-themed clothes and get ready to jump rope! I dressed in **all pink**: a pink T-shirt, a pink tutu with hearts, leggings, and pink heart sneakers. I was so excited because I **love** jump-roping.

We played all kinds of jump rope games to keep our hearts strong. **While jumping, I remembered a verse from the Bible that says to guard our hearts because everything we do flows from them.** Taking care of our bodies is a way to honor God, and staying active is one way to do that!

Now, Let's Reflect

1. What games or activities do you like to play that keep your body healthy?

_____

_____

_____

2. How can you take care of your heart, not just physically but also emotionally and spiritually?

_____

_____

_____

3. What does it mean to honor God with your body?

_____

_____

_____

Prayer

Dear God,
Thank you for giving me a body that can run, jump, and play. Help me take care of my heart and honor You with everything I do. Teach me to be grateful for my health and to encourage my friends to stay healthy, too. Amen.

Roasting S'mores And Scripture

> HOW SWEET ARE YOUR WORDS TO MY TASTE,
> SWEETER THAN HONEY TO MY MOUTH!
> PSALMS 119:103

Have you ever roasted s'mores by a fire pit?

The crackling flames, the gooey marshmallows, and the melted chocolate make it such a fun experience! On the Fourth of July, my cousin AJ and I decided we wanted to do just that. We went to the store and picked out everything we needed—chocolate, crackers, marshmallows, and sticks to roast them over the fire.

AJ was so excited because it was only his second time having s'mores. As he took a big bite, he smiled and said, "These are sweeter than honey to my mouth!" I could tell he really loved them. Spending time with AJ made the day even better. It wasn't just about the tasty treat—it was about creating a memory together. I hope I get to see him in the winter so we can do it all over again.

Moments like this remind me of how God's word is also described as sweeter than honey. Just like the s'mores brought AJ and me happiness, God's Word brings sweetness and joy to our hearts when we take time to read it and think about it.

Now, Let's Reflect

1. Have you ever done something fun with a friend that brought you closer together?

___

___

___

2. How does God's word bring sweetness to your life?

___

___

___

3. What is one way you can share the sweetness of God's love with others?

___

___

___

Prayer

Dear God,
Thank you for the sweet moments we get to share with friends and family. Help us to always appreciate the joy of spending time with others and to find even greater joy in your word. May we share your sweetness with those around us. Amen.

Winning The Spelling Bee: What I Learned

I CAN DO ALL THINGS THROUGH CHRIST WHICH STRENGTHENETH ME.
PHILIPPIANS 4:13

Have you ever been surprised by something you are really good at?

Well, that is what happened to me when I won the spelling bee championship for my class!
 One day, our Language Arts teacher gave us a spelling list to test our ability. I passed the spelling test the first and second times, so she decided to challenge us with even harder words. Most of the kids in my class did not do well, but I passed. That is when she decided to enter me into the spelling bee competition.

Every round, I defeated every member and won the competition for the fifth-grade class! Then they decided to pair me with the middle schoolers. I got knocked out in the third round with the sixth graders when they introduced the word "**DISGRUNTLE.**" It was not part of the advanced-level curriculum spelling words; it was from the easy-level practice. I felt sad that I lost because I thought I was going to win.

Even though I did not sign up to be in the Spelling Bee, I am glad I got the chance because I am a good speller.

Plus, I love to read—I read in the morning before school, at school, and at night. My favorite part of any store is the book section!

Now, Let's Reflect

1. How do you handle it when you do not win something you worked hard for?

_____

_____

_____

2. Why do you think reading and practicing spelling are important skills to have?

_____

_____

_____

3. How can you use your talents, like spelling, to glorify God and help others?

_____

_____

_____

Prayer
Dear God,
Thank you for giving me the talent to spell and read. Help me to stay humble when I win and to learn from my losses. Please guide me to use my gifts in a way that honors you. Amen.

A Glimpse Of God's Creation, Planet Neptune

HE DETERMINES THE NUMBER OF THE STARS AND CALLS THEM EACH BY NAME.
PSALMS 147:4

What was God thinking when creating Neptune?

For the Vocabulary Day Parade, I was given the word Neptune. My job was to be creative and design a costume and a poster board with the word on it. I wanted to make it extra special, so I wrote "Diana Loves Neptune" on my poster and drew a big, blue planet with a smiley face and eyelashes.

Since Neptune has 14 moons, I carefully painted 14 gray moons along the side of my planet, arranging them from largest to smallest. To show that Neptune is an icy planet, I used white ice cream sprinkles to create giant ice rocks! For the strong winds on Neptune, I lightly sketched them with my pencil—I didn't want to make any mistakes.

It was so much fun to create, but it was also hard because I didn't want to mess it up.

I felt a lot of pressure trying to recreate something so amazing that God, my Heavenly Father, had already designed perfectly.

That made me stop and think—can you imagine how much detail God put into creating the entire universe? He didn't just design Neptune but also the other planets, the sun, the moon, and every single star. He carefully painted the sky, placed the stars in just the right spots, and added all the itsy-bitsy details we see in space.

Now, imagine someone asking **YOU** to recreate the whole universe! That's impossible for us, but not for God. His creativity and power are greater than anything we can imagine, and that's why we can always look at his creation with wonder and amazement.

Now, Let's Reflect

1. If you could create your own planet, what would it look like?

_____

_____

_____

2. What's your favorite part of God's creation, and why?

_____

_____

_____

3. How does looking at the stars, moon, and planets remind us of God's greatness?

_____

_____

_____

Prayer
Dear God,
Thank you for creating such an amazing universe filled with planets, stars, and moons. Your design is perfect! Help me to always look at your creation with wonder and remember how powerful and loving you are. Amen.

Seeing The World Like Lord Jesus, Through My Eyeglasses

OPEN MY EYES THAT I MAY SEE WONDERFUL
THINGS IN YOUR LAW.
PSALMS 119:18

My friend Kayla has seen me wearing my glasses every day. She always says I look beautiful in them, which makes me so happy!

One day, just 12 days before Christmas, Kayla asked if she could try on my glasses. I said okay, and she wore them for only a minute before giving them back.

That got me thinking. What if we could look at the world through Lord Jesus' eyes? How long would we last? Would we even make it a minute? Lord Jesus sees everything—the good, the bad, and the things that make him sad. Imagine feeling the weight of seeing people who are hurting, lonely, or in need, just like He does every day.

Sometimes, looking through Lord Jesus' **"lenses"** might feel heavy because it reminds us to care for others, to forgive, and to love unconditionally. But even though it's hard, Lord Jesus gives us strength to see the world as he does and to shine his light in it. This Christmas, let's pray for hearts like his and eyes to see the world with love and compassion.

Now, Let's Reflect

1. How do you think Lord Jesus sees the people around us?

___

___

___

2. What can you do to share his love with someone who might feel sad or lonely?

___

___

___

3. How can you ask Lord Jesus to help you see the world through his eyes this Christmas?

___

___

___

Prayer

Dear Lord Jesus,
Thank you for loving the world so much. Help me to see people the way You do—with love, kindness, and care. Teach me to be patient, to forgive, and to share your light with others, even when it's hard. Amen.

A Girl's Search For Light While Praising God

LET EVERYTHING THAT HAS BREATH PRAISE THE LORD. PRAISE THE LORD.
PSALMS 150:6

On Sunday I created a beautiful artwork called "PRAISE". It features a little girl holding a flashlight as she searches for ways to praise God.

The flashlight in the drawing reminds me that even in the darkest moments, we can always find ways to give God praise. Just like the girl shining her light to find the path, we can use our talents, voices, and hearts to glorify Him every day.

Whether it's through art, helping others, or simply saying "thank you," praising God brings light to the world and joy to our hearts.

Now, Let's Reflect

1. What are some ways you can praise God today?

_____

_____

_____

2. How does praising God bring light to your life and to others?

_____

_____

_____

3. Why do you think it's important to praise God in both happy and difficult times?

_____

_____

_____

Prayer

Dear God,
Thank you for being our guiding light and always showing us reasons to praise you. Help us to look for ways to honor you in everything we do, just like the little girl in the picture. May our lives shine with your love. Amen.

Moses Stuttered Too

> THE LORD SAID TO HIM, "WHO GAVE HUMAN BEINGS THEIR MOUTHS? ... NOW GO; I WILL HELP YOU SPEAK AND WILL TEACH YOU WHAT TO SAY."
> EXODUS 4:11–12

Have you ever been afraid to speak because you worried people wouldn't understand you?

I have been stuttering since I was six years old, and I'm not sure why it started. Sometimes my speech is clear, and other times I stutter—especially when I feel anxious or try to speak too fast. But when I'm doing one of my favorite things—reading out loud to my sister—it disappears.

I've been going to speech therapy and praying about it, and it has gotten better. Then I remembered, I'm not the only one who stutters. God used a great man named Moses, who also stuttered, to lead His people out of Egypt.

Moses told God, "Please forgive me, I have never been good at speaking." He worried that people wouldn't listen because of the way he talked. But God reminded him that He would be with him and help him speak. God even sent Moses' brother, Aaron, to help him.

Moses teaches us that even if we don't speak perfectly, God can still use us to do amazing things.

Now, Let's Reflect

1. Have you ever felt nervous to speak or do something because you thought you weren't good at it?

_____

_____

_____

2. How did God help Moses when he was afraid to speak?

_____

_____

_____

3. What can you do to trust God more when you feel scared or unsure?

_____

_____

_____

Prayer
Dear God,
Thank you for making me just the way I am. Sometimes I feel nervous when I speak, but I know you are with me—just like you were with Moses. Please help me to speak with courage and confidence, and to use my voice to do good things for you. Amen.

True Friendship or Give-Me Friendship

A FRIEND LOVES AT ALL TIMES, AND A BROTHER IS BORN FOR A TIME OF ADVERSITY.
PROVERBS 17:17

Have you ever had a friend who only liked you because of what you could give them?

I have two friends named Sarah and Ella. At first, they were close because Ella promised to give Sarah slime. But guess what? Ella didn't keep her promise. Then, to make up for it, Ella promised glitter and even a pool party! But again, none of these promises happened. Sarah soon realized that Ella's friendship was just full of empty promises. That's when they became **"FRIEND-ENEMIES."**

Sarah told me all about it and asked me to be her friend instead. Now, we have a secret handshake, and I'm happy to be her friend, but I'm not giving her things—just my honest, real friendship. Sometimes, the best friendships aren't about what we give but about being there for each other.

Now, Let's Reflect

1. What do you think makes a real friend?

_____

_____

_____

2. Have you ever had someone promise you something they didn't give? How did that feel?

_____

_____

_____

3. How can you be a good friend to someone else?

_____

_____

_____

Prayer

Dear God,
Thank you for my friends. Help me to be kind, honest, and loving in my friendships. Show me how to be a friend who cares for others, not just for what they give me. Thank you for always being my friend. Amen!

Destiny Challenge Game

> FOR I KNOW THE PLANS I HAVE FOR YOU, DECLARES THE LORD. PLANS TO PROSPER YOU AND NOT TO HARM YOU, PLANS TO GIVE YOU HOPE AND A FUTURE.
> JEREMIAH 29:11

What do you want to be when you grow up?

One day I was playing a game called **Destiny Challenge** with my cousins AJ and EJ. We spread pink, purple, yellow, orange, red, and green papers on the floor. Then we rolled a special color dice that told us which paper to move to. For example, if the dice landed on red, we had to step on the red paper.

As we started, I asked AJ, "What do you want to be when you grow up?" He said, "A football or basketball player." Then I turned to EJ. He also said he wanted to be a football player. I asked him, "Are you sure? Because you have asthma, and running makes it hard for you to breathe. What if God has something else planned for you—like being a teacher, a lawyer, or even a doctor who could find a cure for asthma?"

EJ thought about it and then said, "**Well, since God knows what is best for me, then I agree with Him.**"

That made me realize something important: God controls our destiny. He guides our steps, just like the dice guided our moves in the game. We don't always know when, where, or how we'll get to our future, but God already knows!

So, friends, let me ask you again: What do you want to be when you grow up?

Now, Let's Reflect

1. What do you want to be when you grow up?

_____

_____

_____

2. Why do you think it's important to trust God with your future?

_____

_____

_____

3. How can helping others also be part of reaching your dreams?

_____

_____

_____

Prayer
Dear God,
Thank you for making me special. Please help me to trust your plans for my life. Guide my steps as I grow, and teach me to be kind, loving, and helpful to others. Thank you for always caring for me. Amen.

Taking Care Of My Eyes With God's Help

> THE EYE IS THE LAMP OF THE BODY. IF YOUR EYES ARE HEALTHY, YOUR WHOLE BODY WILL BE FULL OF LIGHT.
> MATTHEW 6:22

Have you ever wondered why your eyes are so important? I do!

Every year, I visit my eye doctor to make sure my eyes are healthy because I have something called **strabismus**. That means my eyes don't always work together, so I need glasses to help me see clearly. My doctor always reminds me to take good care of my eyes by wearing my glasses and not watching too much TV or using my tablet for too long.

If I don't, I might need surgery one day, and that makes me nervous. The worst part is she has to dilate my eye, and everything gets blurry for a while! But I'm learning that God cares about our eyes too, and He helps us take care of them in the best way possible.

Now, Let's Reflect

1. Why do you think it's important to take care of your eyes?

_____

_____

_____

2. How do you feel when your eyes are blurry or hard to see through?

_____

_____

_____

3. What are some things you can do to protect your eyes, just like God wants us to?

_____

_____

_____

Prayer
Dear God,
Thank you for giving me my eyes. Help me to take good care of them and see all the wonderful things you've made. Please keep my eyes healthy, and when I feel scared, remind me that you are always with me. Amen.

God Healed My Eyes!

LORD MY GOD, I CALLED TO YOU FOR HELP, AND YOU HEALED ME.
PSALMS 30:2

Have you ever poked your eye? How did it feel? What did you do to make it better?

Let me tell you what happened to me. In March, the pollen from the trees was really high, making my eyes itchy, watery, and red. It all started when I rubbed my eyes to stop the itch, but it didn't work. Then I scratched them, hoping it would help, but that made it worse! My eyes became very red and irritated.

I told my mom my eyes hurt, so she took me to my eye doctor. He said I had scratches on my cornea and gave us a prescription for Bacitracin eye ointment. We went to four different pharmacies, but none of them had the medicine. We even checked online, but still no luck.

Then Mom said, "Let's wash your eyes with water, kneel down, pray, and ask God for healing." So I did.

The next day, my red eyes were gone! When we saw the doctor two days later, he said, "Your eyes look much better!" I told him we couldn't find the medicine, so we prayed about it.

That day, I learned that when medicine isn't available, God's healing always is! No matter what sickness or problem we face, we can always pray to Him.

Now, Let's Reflect

1. Have you ever been sick or hurt and prayed to God for healing?

_____

_____

_____

2. Why do you think God wants us to pray when we are not feeling well?

_____

_____

_____

3. How can you trust God when things don't go the way you planned?

_____

_____

_____

Prayer

Dear God,
Thank you for being my healer. When I am sick or hurt, help me to trust in You. Thank you for always listening when I pray. Please heal those who are sick and remind them that you love them. Amen.

Hail In Florida?! God Can Do Anything!

> JESUS REPLIED, "WHAT IS IMPOSSIBLE WITH MAN IS POSSIBLE WITH GOD."
> LUKE 18:27

Have you ever seen something that made your jaw drop?

That's exactly what happened to me and my brother Dominick on a hot summer day in Florida. It was 91 degrees outside! We were just having fun together, enjoying some "bro time," when something wild happened.

The sky turned gray. The wind picked up. Then — **ICE CUBES** started falling from the sky! Well... not real ice cubes, but **hail**! Yes, hail in Miami, Florida! We ran to the patio to see it up close. It was cold and bumpy, and we held it in our hands until it melted. There were hundreds—maybe thousands—of tiny frozen balls all over the yard!

Even our neighbors came out with their phones to take videos. None of us had ever seen anything like it. That's when I remembered this awesome verse:

"Jesus replied, "What is impossible with man is possible with God." Luke 18:27

God showed me that day that **He can do the impossible at any time.** If He can make hail fall in hot Miami, He can do anything in your life too!

But the day wasn't over...

Right after the hail, **a big storm hit.** The power went out. **No lights. No Air conditioning.** And worst of all... **no Wi-Fi!** My laptop died. My tablet couldn't connect. Even Dominick's phone wouldn't give me a hotspot.

I was not happy. I felt super frustrated. But then I remembered a Bible story — the one where the disciples were scared in the boat during a storm, and Jesus calmed the sea. I felt like them. Scared. Upset. Tired.

Then I sat down in the chair, breathed deeply, and prayed. We turned on the emergency light and Dominick started goofing off with it, which made me giggle a little and I chased him. And just like that — peace came into my heart. Then, the lights came back on, and the storm passed. God not only calmed the storm outside... He calmed the storm inside me too.

Now, Let's Reflect

1. Have you ever seen something that made you go "Wow, only God could do that"?

_____

_____

_____

2. How do you feel when the power or internet goes out?

_____

_____

_____

3. What can you do when you're feeling upset, scared, or out of control?

_____

_____

_____

Prayer

Dear Lord Jesus,
Thank you for showing me that you can do anything — even make hail fall in sunny Florida! Please help me remember that you're always in control, even when the storms come. Help me trust You when things feel scary or out of control. Calm the storms in my heart and remind me you're always with me. In Jesus' name, Amen.

My First Snow: A Prayer Answered

IF YOU BELIEVE, YOU WILL RECEIVE WHATEVER YOU ASK FOR IN PRAYER.
MATTHEW 21:22

On our way to Washington, DC for our winter vacation, I prayed to God that I would see snow for the very first time in my life.

Our family had plans to visit the Bible Museum, watch the All Creatures Sing Art Show, and have fun in the children's section.

As we drove closer to DC, tiny snowflakes started to fall from the sky. I was so excited that I stuck my tongue out to taste the snow as it gently fell. It tasted cold and felt like tiny pieces of fluffy ice. My prayer was answered!

The snow was so soft, fluffy, and perfectly white—just like I had imagined. Thank God I wore my pink winter jacket, warm socks, and tan boots to keep me cozy and warm.

This moment reminded me that God hears our prayers and answers them in His perfect timing.

Now, Let's Reflect

1. Have you ever prayed for something special and seen God answer it?

_____

_____

_____

2. How did it feel when your prayer was answered?

_____

_____

_____

3. What's something you'd like to pray for this week?

_____

_____

_____

Prayer

Dear God,
Thank you for answering my prayer and letting me see snow for the first time. Help me always trust in you and believe that you hear me when I pray. Amen.

Lost In The Snow: My Phone Gone Forever

> LISTEN TO ADVICE AND ACCEPT DISCIPLINE, AND AT THE END YOU WILL BE COUNTED AMONG THE WISE.
> PROVERBS 19:20

While visiting Washington, D.C., a snow blizzard hit, and I was beyond excited to see the first snow of the year—and hopefully remember it this time!

I geared up with my winter hat, jacket, boots, and gloves. But just before heading out, my mom told me to leave my phone in the house.

The snow was just too exciting, and I couldn't resist the idea of taking pictures and recording my experience. So, I secretly brought my phone along anyway. As soon as I stepped outside, Diana and I jumped into an epic snowball fight. I even tasted the snow—it felt like shaved ice melting on my tongue. Then we headed to the playground to explore in the snow.

By the time we returned to the house, I reached into my pocket and realized... my phone was gone! I searched everywhere for it, but 6 inches of snow had already covered the ground. There was no way I was going to find it now.

Sometimes, even when we think we know better, not listening can have unexpected consequences. Lesson learned—next time, I'll trust my mom's advice!

Now, Let's Reflect

1. Have you ever ignored advice and regretted it later?

_____

_____

_____

2. Why is it important to listen to those who care about us?

_____

_____

_____

3. How can you remind yourself to follow instructions, even when you're excited?

_____

_____

_____

Prayer

Dear God,
Thank you for fun moments like playing in the snow. Help me to listen and follow instructions, even when I'm excited. Teach me to value wisdom and trust those who guide me. Amen.

Rule-Breakers On The Plane

"OBEY THEM THAT HAVE THE RULE OVER YOU, AND SUBMIT YOURSELVES: FOR THEY WATCH FOR YOUR SOULS, AS THEY THAT MUST GIVE ACCOUNT, THAT THEY MAY DO IT WITH JOY, AND NOT WITH GRIEF: FOR THAT IS UNPROFITABLE FOR YOU."
HEBREWS 13:17

On our flight back from Maryland to Florida, the flight attendant reminded everyone to put away their electronics before the plane landed.

I quickly turned off my tablet and put it away, but when I looked to my left, I saw other passengers still watching their phones and tablets. It made me wonder: Why aren't they following the rules?

I asked my mom why those passengers were not listening. She gently explained, "Even if others don't follow the instructions, it's always best to do what's right and follow them yourself." That made me think about how important it is to listen to instructions, even when others don't.

Sometimes, it can feel confusing or unfair when others break the rules and don't face consequences. But doing what is right shows obedience and respect—not just to the people in charge, but also to God.

Now, Let's Reflect

1. Why do you think rules are important, even if others don't follow them?

___

___

___

2. Have you ever been tempted to follow what others are doing instead of doing what's right?

___

___

___

3. How does following instructions show respect to God and others?

___

___

___

Prayer

Dear God,
Thank you for reminding me to listen to instructions and to do what is right, even when others don't. Help me to be obedient and respectful in all situations, knowing that you see my heart and actions. Amen.

We Were Stuck On The Plane: Trusting God's Perfect Timing

THE LORD IS GOOD TO THOSE WHOSE HOPE IS IN HIM, TO THE ONE WHO SEEKS HIM..
LAMENTATIONS 3:25

On our way back from Washington, D.C., we were beyond excited to finally return home.

Our flight had already been delayed for two days because of a snowstorm, and the idea of being back in Florida sounded amazing. But when we landed, there was another problem—there wasn't an open gate for our plane to park!

We had to sit on the plane for another hour and a half, waiting patiently while three other flights deplaned ahead of us. It was frustrating, but in moments like that, I'm reminded that God's timing is always perfect. When it's not your time or season, God might hold you back—not to punish you, but to prepare you for what's next.

Eventually, it was our turn. The plane finally reached a gate, and we were able to grab our luggage and head home. God's delays are never wasted; they're part of His plan to guide us and teach us patience.

Now, Let's Reflect

1. Have you ever experienced a delay that frustrated you at first? What did you learn from it?

___

___

___

2. Why do you think God sometimes makes us wait for things we want?

___

___

___

3. How can you trust God's timing, even when it's hard to be patient?

___

___

___

Prayer

Dear God,
Thank you for teaching me patience and reminding me that your timing is always perfect. Help me to trust you in the delays and know that You are working everything for my good. Amen.

FAVORITE MEMORY VERSE PAGE

www.ingramcontent.com/pod-product-compliance
Lightning Source LLC
Chambersburg PA
CBHW071630040426
42452CB00009B/1572